THE PERFECT
BASTARD

THE PERFECT BASTARD

POEMS

QUINN CARVER JOHNSON

CURBSTONE BOOKS / NORTHWESTERN UNIVERSITY PRESS
EVANSTON, ILLINOIS

Curbstone Books
Northwestern University Press
www.nupress.northwestern.edu

Printed in the United States of America

10 9 8 7 6 5 4 3 2 1

Library of Congress Cataloging-in-Publication Data

Names: Johnson, Quinn Carver, author.
Title: The perfect bastard : poems / Quinn Carver Johnson.
Description: Evanston : Curbstone Books/Northwestern University Press, 2023.
Identifiers: LCCN 2023012906 | ISBN 9780810146501 (paperback) | ISBN 9780810146518 (ebook)
Subjects: LCGFT: Poetry.
Classification: LCC PS3610.O3723 P47 2023 | DDC 811.6—dc23/eng/20230316
LC record available at https://lccn.loc.gov/2023012906

To my mom, Kelly, the constant moon in my life.

&

*To Woody Guthrie—let's show these fascists
what a couple of hillbillies can do!*

CONTENTS

[ACT III]

[ACT IV]

THE PERFECT BASTARD

A Prediction // A Spoiler

Right now, in the locker room, a punk kid is trembling as they lace up their boots, probably vomiting in their own duffel bag. My God. Thought they had grown up, thought just because they could roll with a few punches, they could handle the rough-n-tumble. Sure, they stood here, took a couple nasty chops, kept their spine straight, grimaced, never looked away, but that's only half the story. What you in the stands didn't see, what they didn't consider, was the next morning—oh hell that next morning—waking up on that crackerboard mattress in that roach motel, feeling the redness in their chest before they even open their eyes. That kid is making their way to the ring right now—out of the makeshift dressing room, down the empty hall, through the swinging double doors leading into the armory ballroom, on their way out here to collect enough bruises & broken bones to make your $15 ticket worthwhile. A kid who just realized they're still a child. A kid who realized you can't just stitch *This Machine Kills Fascists* into the soles of your boots & drop-kick the world. It's not that simple. The world gets back up & throws a mean punch. In this business, they say when your time comes, you go out on your back / you can't take it with you / don't be a hero / all that bullshit. It sounds good, doesn't it? But it's all air & empty champagne flutes, the promises made to you. No, you people don't want poetry, you want blood. You want what you paid for & we're here to entertain you, send you home happy. So here's the deal—the kid's gonna come through those curtains with a heart full of integrity & march their way into this ring & demand what has always been theirs &

that kid is going to die out here.

The Territory

The Midwest. The Mid-South. Kansas. Oklahoma. Arkansas. Missouri.
Outer space. Small towns. High school gymnasiums. Armories. Banquet halls.
Ballrooms. Makeshift dressing Rooms. Roach motels. Highways. Backstreets.
Today.

The Roster

The Perfect Bastard *(they/them)*: The hero of our story. The villain in the ring. A child. An adult. A wrestler. A jobber. A bastard. A queer.

The Moon *(she/her)*: A mother. The moon.

Sammy *(he/him)*: A child. A son. A friend. A source of regret.

The First Crusher *(he/him)*: An opponent. A potential lover.

The Sunset Kid *(he/him)*: A cowboy. A radical. A mentor. A partner. A lover. An outlaw.

Tanner Hart *(she/her)*: A champion. A valet. A girlfriend. A wife. A friend. A cautionary tale.

Jack Holiday *(he/him)*: The shiniest puppet. A henchman to the villain. A hero in the ring. A shining smile on your TV screen. The champion.

The Executioner *(he/him)*: A henchman to the henchman. A class traitor. A company guy. A scab. The axe. The gavel.

Adrian Street *(he/him)*: A son. A father. A father figure. A husband. A champion. A role model. An inspiration. Ahead of his time. A straight man playing queer. An embodiment of Middle America's queer panic. A scapegoat. A punching bag. A punch line. Outdated even in his own time.

Terry Taylor *(he/him)*: A former champion. The strong arm of Middle America's queer panic. Leader of the charge. A victim. A violent man. A man's man. An emasculated man. Failed by America's queer panic. A scapegoat. A discarded pawn. The strong arm of American Panic. Once and future champion.

The Puppeteer *(he/him)*: The booker. The boss. The boardroom. The money. The Invisible Hand. The Puller of Strings. The real villain of our story. The final word.

[ACT I]

The Birth of the Perfect Bastard

[A MYTHOLOGY]

demigod—
a man, drunk,
blasts
shotgun stars
into space,
craters
the moon,
patron saint
of change
& lost
queers.
She falls
for him,
crashes
through
the decay
already
rotting
his roof.
On earth,
she doesn't
shift
or trans-
form to
human—
just remains
luminous orb
floating
in the room
or turns into
a pack
of stray dogs,
hunger
hot
slick
on their
tongues.

Still,
in a heap
of insulation
& chimney
soot
the moon
pulls
the tides
up over
the man
& beneath
the covers
she gives
birth. A bastard,
their father
called them.
The bastard
daughter
of the sun
called them
her own,
perfect.
Cradling
the child
she says,
This baby
of ours
will cycle
through
seasons
like their
mother,
beauty
every time,
but
they have
your blood
too—

this baby
born of
bourbon
sweat &
spit
tobacco.
Their
heart
a tin can
tethered
by string,
always
calling,
vibrating
desire.

Before It Sets In

When I was six
maybe, one of the older boys
in the neighborhood slipped a tree branch
between the spokes of my bike, sent me
careening into loose gravel. Someone else
might tell you this was the moment
they learned they could tolerate pain. Not me.
I cried the whole dizzy run home. I'm not sure
I ever had that moment. I'm not sure anyone has.

I spend most evenings
sweating over the fight to come &
the whole night after pulsing in agony. Only
those few, untethered moments in the ring
are free of worry, when I buzz like static,
my muscles on autopilot,
slap the mat to rile up the crowd
& launch myself over the top rope, the fight spilling
out into the arena. But that's a different story. No,

the lesson came from my mother.
A trinket of wisdom passed
through a lineage of resourceful women
from mother to daughter to granddaughter
to rest finally in the hands of this perfect, bastard child—
your own saliva can pull a bloodstain from fabric.

I sat, crying in the bathroom,
as my mother made me spit & spit
into my splattered shirt—*I can't do it,*
she said, *it has to come from you—*
as my mother dabbed stinging alcohol
into splotches & smears of scrapes.
Quick. Before it sets in.

Then it's too late. Slowly,
the small dark something
that had blotted the fabric began to fade.
The magic, to make the evidence of pain
disappear. To transform the body
using only the body. To negate & replenish.

Now, after each match, I sit in the damp, barely light
of converted storage rooms & spit into my gear,
scrubbing from it the night's gruesome history.
With each swish of the cheeks, pucker of the lips,
scrutiny of the thumb & forefinger,
pulling molecules of myself from the weaving.

When I'm not alone on the road,
I sit shotgun in the harsh beam
of the overhead cabin lights
& perform the post-match ritual.
Spit. Scrub. Spit. Scrub. Driving through
the night & at the crack of a new day,
all memory of one town erased
just as I reach the next.

Of course, it is therapy to wash away
what brings us pain. Therapy to start
again the next morning, new & clean.

The Beauty of the Backyard Wrestling League

is that all of us are the champion of something
& we carry our respective titles, fashioned
from cardboard, duct tape & thick-tipped markers,
around our shoulders everywhere we go.
Logan wore his on the playground once & someone
from the rec center wrestling team put him
in a real full nelson just to prove a point.
Logan only brings his belt to the matches now.

Tonight, I am the champion of the kickout,
no one can keep my shoulders to the grass for three.
I am the champion of the duck & weave,
the patron saint of survival, of running away.
Sammy is the champion of the trampoline,
of the large backyard, of cream soda in the fridge.
The champion of high-flying,
of throwing himself around the yard,
off the tops of fence posts.
Logan is the champion of the shin kick
& now Wyatt is the champion
of limping in circles, but soon he will be
the champion of the comeback.

Wyatt had a birthday last week, which means
his belt is shiny, golden plastic on foam strap—
He is the champion of birthdays—but Sammy's Dad
is the one we all really admire.

Sammy's Dad keeps a glass cabinet in the hall
filled with $1,000 replicas of all the real belts,
the ones we watched John Cena & Triple H wear on TV,
the belts he watched The Rock & Bret Hart carry,
cast in real metal with real leather straps.
Sammy's Dad won't let us touch the belts,
not even his son, but we spend hours
in front of the case, tilting our heads to watch
the light glint off what we think must be real gold.

But remember I'm the champion of kickouts,
& now Sammy has gotten frustrated, climbed
to the top of a plastic pool ladder, & dropped
an elbow, like a blade, right into my sternum,
so I'm out of breath on the back steps
when I hear the call in the living room—Sammy's Dad
getting called into work late, driving off in his truck.

I'm by the back door. The boys are tangled up
in their own fight. So I slip inside, careful
not to let the screen slam behind me.
I slide the glass open. The belts

are colder than you would expect, almost painful
to the touch, my palms slick with sweat.
But I was out of breath, hurting
from the elbow taken earlier, remember, so I had no choice.
I was the champion of survival.

& the belt was so cold, that's what Sammy said
after he turned at the wrong moment &
I crashed the metal plate into his nose. Of course,
he cried & cried & bled all over the yard
& I pulled *sorry* from my throat like a clown's
handkerchief, tied to another *sorry* & they just
kept coming up. Of course, we tried to wash
the blood off the center plate & of course,
we tried to put the belt back right where it had been
& of course, we never said anything about it again.

Tonight I have been crowned
the champion of something unnameable
that cannot be scrubbed clean.

Ode to the Hometown Crowd

The night before, the Perfect Bastard dreamt
a full moon, an arena filled with family & friends,
with people who loved them for what they carried
beneath the paint job. In the dream, the years away
had transformed the town into the *Home of the Perfect Bastard*,
not just road signs & a painted water tower, but
a place where they could really belong. In the crowd, a sign read
HOME IS WHERE THE HEART IS except
the heart was just a symbol for the heart
& another just said WELCOME HOME & in their dream
they knew who held the sign, but when they woke,
they couldn't remember. By then it didn't matter.
The sign was gone. The day had come.

⸕

On the car ride in, passing old schools
& old restaurants with new names, they pull off
onto a side road, drive out to the local hiking trail.

Veering off the well-marked path, they duck
under branches, crawl through a tunnel
tighter than they remember until they stand up

inside the foundational walls of an old cement factory,
where teenagers first discovered cigarettes &
beer & bodies. In the dirt, a few cans of paint.

The Perfect Bastard shakes the bottles until
one works. Next to the names of prom royalty
& quarterbacks & outlaw poets they scrawl

Return of the Perfect Bastard   Below that
they read *back-to-back state champs*
& they picture a pristine championship belt

next to the football trophies & golf plaques &
debate medals in the glass case. They smile
on the slow, sauntering walk back to the car.

Beneath the waves of a massive American flag,
blotting out the sun, a tube man flutters his arms
in the breeze. Beneath that, the Perfect Bastard
stands outside for a meet&greet, smiling
at passersby shopping for more seats,
better safety options. A man stops at the table
with the glossy 8 × 10s, says *My son*
used to watch all this stuff. Back when he was a kid.
Even had this group who rolled around in the backyard.
He grew out of it all, of course. But I'll ask
if he's ever heard of you. Can I take your picture?   *click / snap*

⁓

The Perfect Bastard walks down
into the VFW banquet hall to watch the crew assemble the ring,
to watch them pull canvas taut like concrete &
stretch it over the wooden baseboards. Next week, a few
will need repaired / replaced, but this week they'll suffice;
the Perfect Bastard makes a mental note to avoid
taking bumps in the northern corners of the ring.

The crew—
the regular road workers, shouting orders, & some eager-eyed teenagers
wanting to feel the ring real in their hands, offering
their help to get just a little closer to the action.
Tonight, these boys will sit up high in the nosebleeds,
but right now, each one of them can imagine
how it must feel to stand on the turnbuckles &
raise their hands to a chorus of love.

When the Perfect Bastard
looks into their eyes, they can see each boy
climbing the ladder, making himself famous,
each boyhood dream finally realized, the drop
to the knees, the kiss on the gold plate of the belt,

the tears & in the audience more tears. Beat-red chest,
welts rising on the back, swelling in the ankles,
the commentary team is crying too, repeating
the same lines about the hard-fought war,
how each of these boys left it all in the ring. Left it all
in the ring. The Perfect Bastard hears the music, feels
the shredding confetti dropping, they sway with the pan
& zoom of the camera, the instant replay,
the set & lock on the champion

                          & the Perfect Bastard
imagines the crown, the sash, the scepter, the flash
of the local camera, the caption: *Homecoming*
but they've let their own dreams take hold now.
They are not the eager boys assembling the ring
& those boys are not even the boys they dream of being.

⁓

The Perfect Bastard looks around the armory ballroom,
wishes they had a memory of the place before tonight.

Something sweet. Maybe
they used to see the matches here.
Sat high on someone's shoulders
for a better view. Cheered
loudly for the babyfaces. Booed
the heels 'til they lost their voice.
Nothing comes to them
& they aren't sure they've ever
been inside this building,
except for graduation maybe.
Or homecoming.

⁓

Later that night, under the full moon,
the Perfect Bastard slowly walks out
of the locker room, down to the ring,
yellow & white & purple & black
ribbons fluttering from their biceps,
streams of blue & pink & white
flowing from their eyes.
They crack their knuckles, looking at
their tattooed fingers, dollar-store nails,
& they are grateful to conceal their face
beneath the streaks of paint. They scan
the small crowd for the boys from earlier,
hope they found seats closer to the front—
the ones where you can pat a wrestler
on the back as they head to the ring—
but can't find them anywhere.
                              Then,
walking, foaming plastic cup of beer in hand,
toward an empty seat—a woman on one side,
on the other, a screaming child in an opponent's T-shirt—
is a face the Perfect Bastard once saw

                              in their dream? behind
                              a cardboard sign?
No,
not there. On a gravel street, holding a tree branch.
In a hallway, meaty palm slapping a locker shut.
On a turf field, helmet in hand, hair flowing down the neck.
No, not there either
& then the face is gone
the man sitting in his seat,
chugging his beer, cheering
with his child &
he's a stranger again.

                              ⤝

When the Perfect Bastard
comes back to the ring,
they're on the top rope,
bruised limbs & blood tinting
their face paint just beneath
the right eye, lifted up on a man's shoulders
like a father holding a kid to see better,
& then they're on their back,
a hard crack somewhere in the body
or below it & as the ref counts
the refrain, they look out
& see no signs, no ghosts,
no eager-eyed boys,
just another crowd.

Cheap Heat // Action City

& in the midwest

on my drag down Main / out for lunch / I count more abandoned buildings / than not / & through the dust-tinted storefront window / I guess that the gallery filled with mattresses / sold them / once / outside grizzled men / sit on the sidewalk / beneath a ripped awning / that once shielded summer sun / next door / a bookstore has moved to a new location / at the new location / a bookstore / has closed / SORRY / outside the family-owned vacuum shop / stands Bigfoot in overalls / some say it's a front for drugs / how many vacuums can you possibly sell / they always say / Bigfoot in the parking lot / *come in* / Bigfoot in the window / a warning / *don't come asking any questions* / on the drive down dirt roads / trailers turned to homes / turned to laboratories / have turned to ashes / on the corner / a church sign / *we have two bathrooms* / *gen 5:2* / on the road into town / billboard / MAGA / VOTE RED / back alley / behind the 1920s vaudeville theater / teenage graffiti / LOVE MORE / PLEASE

& in the midwest

I come spinning / screaming / from town to town / like a tornado / I can pack the whole county into the seats / in the basement gym of the old 2A high school / huddled beneath the handsewn banners of titles / long since surrendered / in towns where there is little more to do / than break what is not yours / to break / people cannot take their eyes off / the mess / I leave in my wake / & when I come spiraling / through the sky / shattering glass panes & breaking bodies over boards / mothers curtain their hands / over their children's eyes / but they peek through / fingers like plastic blinds / dads drink beers / to celebrate the wreckage / as if / this kind of disaster is nothing out of the ordinary / & you can read about it in the local paper / tomorrow / an opinion column / a concerned parent / what will this do to her two young boys / to see this type of pain / this violence / where they call home

The Perfect Bastard Finds a Photograph of Adrian Street & His Father

I found you as a teenager, deep in the pages of a magazine
pulled from the dusty cardboard archive beside the VHS tapes.
I found you, still radiant blue in black&white. Even then,
I could see what they never could: the men in the mines.
Your father. Adrian, what did he say? When you left
in work boots & returned in platform heels, towering?
Not one of them looks down at you. Not anymore.
They crane their necks in the picture—coalblacksoot
wiped from the eyes just to squint in your light. Adrian,
what is transformation but growing taller than all that
denies your worth?
                                    I spent hours looking at your photo,
long flowing robe, lips a shade of silver or gold. You
are royalty, crowned & crying lightning bolts. You write
a new history & pose next to the old one. Men crawl out
of holes in the ground for you. How could it be, Adrian,
that you should be next to your father, in front of the mines,
black & white & blue & silver & worth your weight in gold
& even then he couldn't love you? Not the way I love you.
All of them, just a lot of pissant men. Short men. Tiny frail men.
There are a million men like that. Adrian, there is only you. &
someday, maybe, me.

The words they said to you: *Isn't she cute?* / *Give us a kiss*. Empty.
Even with headlamps shining these men glow dim next to you
& it shows. Their screams filled seats in the stands, booed your matches.
Their echo hasn't stopped bouncing off cave walls & arena
rafters. I know because I can hear it when I wake in pools of sweat.
I hear it in the grocery store. In line at the bank. At the red light.
When someone throws words like bricks & they barely miss me.
I catwalk in my bedroom. Pose in the mirror. Dream of being you.
But in grocery lines, I cross my arms, stare at my shoelaces, try
not to make eye contact with anyone. When I give the woman
at the register a handful of crumpled bills, I try to hide
my neon-painted nails. I look out the storefront window.
Inspect the checkout displays of gum & celebrity gossip.
Avoid her eyes as she deposits coins back into my colorful hands.
But then I watch as you pick up the brick, stamp it with a kiss
& chuck it back.

We Want Tables

[A CHORUS OF COAL MINERS,
CONSTRUCTION WORKERS
& CUSTODIANS]

We want to feel the swing
of the hammer's fist, swell of the backstroke
rolling into the big wave on the way down,
knocking us on our asses. We want to feel gravity—
no theory, just the way bodies move & then
stop moving. Brick wall, ya know. That feeling.
We want just the moment itself—nothing
before or after. We're tired of context,
all day long, so we buy the ticket &
the marked-up cheap beer & for a few hours
you're going to strip
everything of its context. We want tables
without the set dressing—just hard wood
& four legs. We don't want
the platonic ideal of anything. Chairs
that no one sits in & that's realer than life.
Tonight, we want to feel hungry—
& we don't want you to feed us.
No, we want to starve up here
in the nosebleeds. Yes,
we want nosebleeds. Sprain your ankle.
Keep dancing. Dislocate. Decontextualize.
Ring your bell & let us hear it echo.
We want to watch your eyes roll back
into your head. We don't want to see you cry—
happy or sad.

Puppet Show

Children gather 'round the castle-shaped box
to watch the toys dance on their strings. Almost
invisible in the right light, it's easy to pretend
they've come to life, easy to prism a single voice

into several, to construct conversation from monologue.
Jack Holiday is the shiniest puppet with the shiniest
puppet belt. The writhing fingers love him the most,
give him the best lines. Let him slay all the dragons

& vanquish hordes of all the other goblin puppets.
All the children tug at sleeves, beg leather wallets
to empty themselves in the name of Jack Holiday.
Behind the curtain, the hands collect all the money

into a single pile, scattering some loose coins   &   getting smaller smaller
our direction & tucking a crisp $20 bill   in the pocket of the world champion.

[A NOTE TUCKED INTO THE PERFECT BASTARD'S DUFFEL BAG]

what's a champion?
the guy who smiles nicest
on late-night talk shows,
poses prettiest for pictures?
who crowns the champ?
the ref? the fans?
a boardroom of marketing execs?
we go out each night & throw
these top guys to the moon
& who wraps us in gold?
they won't even pay
to fill our teeth with it.

—sunset

Tanner Hart Burns

Tanner Hart, wearing the championship belt,
comes to the ring, accompanying her kayfabe boyfriend,
the Ponca City Cyclone. Cheering him on in his match.
This is her only angle tonight & she'll repeat the process.

In every town, she'll walk, belt glistening, trailing behind
a mid-card talent who can work, sure, everyone agrees, but
lacks it on the mic. Far from the main event picture.
His opponent is the Executioner, industry veteran stepping
back in the squared circle, hoping to give a few kids
some momentum on his way out. The Axe is clearly superior
in the ring, but loses anyway & Hart smiles for the camera.

Hart yearns to fight. Hart strains toward the ring.
When she laces her boots backstage, straps the gold
heavy around her waist, holds the ropes open
for the Cyclone, Hart feels the pulse of the crowd
vibrating through the wires. Hart wants it. Hart breaks

bodies in sparring classes, but even with cameras off
she's lucky to prowl the outside, play some part
in the finish. When she leaps on the apron to distract
the ref, when she throws a low-blow kick while no one
(except fans & phone cameras) is watching, Hart feels
the static in her soles. When they hand her the mic

long enough to hurl a teenage boy's insult at an opponent's
girlfriend's alleged roster of boyfriends, the mic feels
like a steel chair. You can only hurt one person at a time
with a steel chair, but you can swing a microphone
at the exposed back of an entire audience, swing it
like a hammer through camera lenses & soundboards,

into the boardrooms of promoters & broadcasters,
crashing into offices of in-house doctors &
on-retainer lawyers. She says her line. She kicks
an opponent in the metaphors. She kisses her man.
Her gold hangs heavy.

In bigger cities or tapings, Hart cuts a promo
before the match. Asks the Executioner's wife to step
in the ring with her, to challenge her for the belt, but,
of course, she doesn't. *It makes good TV,* the wife tells her

backstage. *My friends called. Scared for me. Thought you might snap
me in half for real.* The wife laughs her way out of the room
& Hart looks for the punch line, wonders if it's concealed

beneath layers of lean muscle or obscured by the glint
of light on her golden belt. She knows, of course, that's the joke.
Tanner Hart wants to step in the ring, sweat mascara
down her cheeks, come home bruised. When the Cyclone throws
a spinning elbow into the meaty bicep of his opponent,
Hart scouts her own elbow crashing into jawbone.
When he takes a lariat & stays standing, it seam-rips the crowd
but Hart knows he's just working stiff, has his footing wrong.
Sloppy suplex. Botched bucklebomb. Misplaced machete chops.

The checks come—lots of appearances, no injuries & it's almost
good money. Paid to stand there & let someone else take the beating
so why, the wife's book club asks in unison, *would she want
to get her hands dirty in the ring?*

Hart calls home, vents to her wife, stares at the belt—
neon leopard strap, gaudy pink heart centerplate,
studded with rainbow rhinestones & she wants
to toss it off a bridge, to hear that *ploink*
before it settles into the sand below. She imagines
the soft beat of that pink heart bubbling in the water,
another entry on a list of unexplained sounds,
a mystery only Hart knows the answer to.
Let them have the champion of catfish, she thinks,
if they don't care about me. But she doesn't.

Ponca texts: *wearing green tonight. please find something
to match.* She straps the belt back around her waist. Hart plays
her role. Sweep the opponent's legs on the mat. Distract the ref.
Belt shot to the head. Whatever it takes for this man to win.
After the bell, Hart raises his arm in victory & kisses him
for all the cameras, all the families watching at home.

Intimacy Suplex

we all did it because of Shawn Michaels:
we put the metal ring through the tender part
that once connected us to life & pre-life

heartbroken, all the kids wanted to be
the Heartbreak Kid back in his glory days
we imagined descending from the rafters
like zebra-print angels   we all heard
the sweet crack of the kick, a body
crashing through panes of sugar glass

gloves / sterile needle / hot fluorescent
the doctor ties the cord into a knot &
snip   a balding man, mid-thirties, slips
a long, cold needle through the scar

it's mostly anticipation, mostly long inhales
& sharp exhales   *just a quick sting*   close
your eyes, tuck your chin & fall to the mat

belly-to-belly, in the center of the ring,
a man clasps you between his shoulders
& snaps you into the mat   long inhale
mostly   but something in that second snags

feel that, warm like liquid in your gut
like fire spreading slowly, red wet palms
& there tangled in a man's chest hair
a dangling glimmer of sterling silver

look & see your own cluttered debris
attached to a body that isn't yours
& the cut tether, the severed connection

& alone now you are reborn just as you were born:
out of flesh & blood, you are reshaped
& you do not walk away without a scar

The Perfect Bastard vs. the First Crusher

They lock collars & elbows together,
tie two bodies into one until it breaks
or becomes something more beautiful.

It feels like they are dancing & it's hard
for the Perfect Bastard not to smile,
to close their eyes & feel the sway

of these two bodies drifting together
& apart like tides. They feel a hand,
firm, on their hip & they feel alive—

like they want to shiver from cold
or heat. It has only been a few seconds
maybe, but it feels longer.

No, the Perfect Bastard thinks,
it doesn't feel like time has passed at all.
They feel like time has dropped away

& only space is left, only distance.
There is, in all this space, an arena
full of bodies but they are dropping

away now too, like the opposite of the wave,
like the whole crowd is sitting down, row by row
& falling, like a reverse ripple, toward

a center point. The whole universe
is a twenty-by-twenty-foot square
& contains only the Perfect Bastard
& their opponent. The Perfect Bastard
thinks *opponent* is too harsh a word.

They prefer *partner* but
need to ask first.

The Perfect Bastard wants to read him poetry
written specifically for him. They want to say,
It's okay. Leave the lights on.

The Perfect Bastard hears church bells
& angels singing & for once, this doesn't
seem melodramatic.

He puts the Perfect Bastard in a sleeper hold
& for a brief moment they feel
like they might actually fall asleep—

Not pass out like you're supposed to. No,
actually, truly, peacefully fall asleep.

The Perfect Bastard imagines themselves as the big spoon,
but they know deep down they are the little spoon.
The crowd also knows they are the little spoon.

The crowd is watching the match after all. The match,
it occurs to them, is already over & they are the loser.
At some point, there was a ring bell & the crowd

erupting into boos or cheers.

[NOTE]

harsh irony:
they book us in the smoke break match
& we're the ones who need a light

practical magic:
slap nicotine patches
under your KT tape
& let your opponent
knock you light-headed
good kind of dizzy
under those big bright lights

—sunset

In the Alley between Matches, the Sunset Kid Explains the History of Cigarettes

you ever heard that story
folks like us used to roll up
what's left of the rich man's cigar
& the cigarette was born
that's our history   what we do—
take what's thrown away
& make it all we own
collect in buckets
what trickles
down to
us

you ever worked a desk job
yeah, of course   think about
how you picked up this habit
just to get a five-minute break
we trade years for minutes
while the Booker holds maduros
in his invisible hand, deposits ashes
in a crystal tray

—hand me that beer can
stamp this out on my boot &
save it for later   look   last in the pack
that's the lucky one   big match tonight
jobbing for the top guy

꩜

In a box of mementos,
the Perfect Bastard finds

a plastic-wrapped cigarillo,
IT'S A BOY stamped in blue.

That night, sore & tired, they
roll a blunt with the wrap—

slide the switchblade across
the seam, spilling the poison guts

& filling the body with what
has always served it best,

the lick, the tender sealing
of the wound—

Their friends need no
explanation or occasion

—the rebirth, the reveal.

Ode to the Pink Cowboy Hat

& in the summer of 1986,
"I Wanna Be a Cowboy"
was No. 12 on the charts

& the music video featured
a man, a *best of the bad* type,
buck naked except his hat,
smoking a blunt in the bath

& MTV hated the video—
said it *wasn't rock 'n' roll*—
but the song was a smash hit
so they had no choice

& that's how it found me
two decades later: a child
discovering the last remnants
of VHS tapes in their room

as the cartoon thought bubble
begins to expand, learning
that a fantasy looks like
a naked cowboy in his bathtub

& that was the summer of 2006
but in the summer of 1986
Boys Don't Cry released
their only major hit song

& during that same summer,
& that summer only,
Bob Orton wore a pink hat
when he came to the ring
alongside the adorable one,
when visiting Adrian Adonis
in the Flower Shop, when
bludgeoning his old friend
Roddy Piper in the ring

& it's telling that Lemmy Kilmister
plays a spaghetti western cowboy
in the video for "I Wanna Be a Cowboy"
& I watched those old westerns
in the boxes of VHS tapes

& it's telling that in those films
the hero wears the white hat,
rides into town on a white stallion
to gun down the villain beneath
the midnight brim

& I don't need to tell you
what it means that "Cowboy"
Bob Orton came to the ring
in a pink hat, paired with
Adonis's lace & eye shadow

& I don't need to tell you
who the villain of the story was
or who was gunned down
when Roddy Piper decided
that a town wasn't big enough
for two men

but what I need to tell you is
I can make a town or a home
big enough for two men

All it takes is a small garden
in the windowsill—here,
take this spade, gather me
a handful of soil from the park
& I could plant seeds in the ground,
beg rain from the clouds, turn
Piper's Pit into the Flower Shop

I would tug at lavender leaves &
draw you a bath, roll the herb tight,
& add mint to your tea

if you're going to be a cowboy
then I wanna be a cowboy too
& I want to wear the pink hat

[ACT II]

Nightfall // Daybreak,
or The Last Ride of the Sunset Kid

The first time the Perfect Bastard kisses a boy
is in front of their parents. The school play.
Frantic, book in hand, they review their lines
quick & run through the curtain, instantly beamed
with sweat under the hot, direct lights, directly
into the arms of a boy & lose their voice.
Line: someone speaks. & then: a kiss. Cheers,
maybe. Did someone weep? A door, somewhere
in the back of the room clicks closed but
the Perfect Bastard doesn't look out to the seats
they know may now be empty. Backstage:
warm against the cold concrete dressing room.
Costume suits thrown over racks, neckties
ripped from their knots. A door, somewhere.
A door lock. *Click.* Press the weight of the body
against it. Just in case—

      Sunset appears in the window

carrying two stuffed duffels & grinning like daybreak
himself. He throws his bags into the back & runs back
up to the porch of his duplex. Rips down a string of fly tape.
Stuffs it into the bin by the curb. In the passenger seat
he says, *If you're gonna kill us / just kill us.* He swats
imaginary flies, palm crack on the dash. *Hell no.*
They set traps / now it's our fault. He stretches
a strip of KT tape over his shoulder blade, has them
smooth down a section he can't reach, near the curve
of his spine. *Puppeteer says I'm cleared to compete.*
He locks up with the air. A pull, a wince, a falter.
I'd argue, but rent's due / doctors' bills piled up
like magazines on the coffee table. The Perfect Bastard
turns the key & the rental car bounces down the highway

toward St. Louis tonight. Tomorrow Springfield.
Jeff City. Two nights in KC. Cross the river,
then U-turn. North of Topeka. West of the 71.
Head north. Different Springfield,
but they'll cut the same promo to heat up the crowd.

The Kid & the Perfect Bastard are in a tag team now—
The Perfect Sunsets—so they run the road in the daylight
& run the ropes in the evenings. Beat down / hot tag /
drop-kick / Irish whip / running tackle / tag / two bodies
lift a third / hook under the legs / support the back /
double power bomb on the mat / pin. In one city,
they're brothers. In another, childhood friends.
But always they move as one, drop perfect kicks
into the guts of other teams.

In the car, the Perfect Bastard pulls out a set of action figures
& on the dashboard, they plan extravagant finishes—
a sunset flip from the top of a tower of doom
or a moonsault countered into a Bastard Bomb.
Sunset says he'll teach them the flip, how to throw
their momentum like a gyroscope at the exact moment,
how to press an opponent's body into the mat
with enough force. The Perfect Bastard formulates
a modified Bastard Bomb at the end of the rotation
& maps out stereo Perfect Sunset Bombs, in sync
right in the middle of the ring.

In the car, they talk sports / politics /
dream jobs / jobless dreams. The Kid says,

The Booker running this show's got
money in his right & strings in the left
& he's got more than he can hold both ways.
More money than he could spend in a lifetime
& we've got more lifetimes than we can afford
so we beat each other to pulp for spare change
& he blames our hearts for bleeding.
Say you go out in the ring & twist your ankle,
pull muscle right off the bone / or worse.

Now you're out six weeks, at least. Six weeks
with no checks, but the rent doesn't stop,
the lights start going out, the water dries up
evaporates in the faucet & you have to pay
the doctor just to get your ankle suitable enough
to step back in there & break yourself down again.
                                        Jack Holiday
breaks his body clean in two & he's got
the best doctors in the state making sure
he can go back out the next week & defend
the company belt. I jobbed for him two months back
& he could barely walk—torn tendon. I had to
carry him through the whole match just so he could
limp away with the winner's purse.

If I had a hammer   I'd swing at the bookers
& the crooks   If we had steel chairs & bolt cutters
we could free ourselves, but it's all distraction
They hang gold above our heads & we fight
our way up the ladder   If I had a ladder
I'd climb up & up & jump right back down,

        drop
            a
              big elbow

                    take the whole back office with me.

But it's no use. Neither of us are moving the needle,
out in the ring or not. You start pulling back
on those strings & you'll just get cut loose,
but if we could knot all those little threads together,
braid them up into some thick rope & give it
a firm tug we could pull the whole foundation down.

[NOTE, WRITTEN WITH CARE]

Out there, it's all babyfaces & heels,
but we all know that back here it's
jobbers & champions: top of the ladder
& the ladder itself. No,
even that's a distraction. Really
it's jobbers & the bookers, the invisible hand
& his action figures. The champ's just
the guy they suckered into thinking
he's special. Put a fake belt on some fool
& he'll think he won it all himself.
Look at Holiday, in his private room
drinking chardonnay. He won't lie down
& get pinned clean because he thinks it's real,
thinks he's the champion of something tangible.
He's not any different than we are,
here in the communal storage closet,
but we've got enough sense to see it.
So picture this:

hold the ring
in your hands
like a jar &
then let it fall
listen to the crash
of glass on concrete

leave the ring empty
& shattered, spill
the locker room out
on the sidewalk

let the sand gather
in plain view, piling
into a heap beyond
the grains & let
the boardroom
find the glue & paste
to repair the shards

see now how the beauty
of this act glitters in the

—sunset

Out on the circuit, the pair find themselves
parked at a hole-in-the-wall in a tiny town
just off the interstate. The midnight manager
says the only vacancies are singles, but
the sofa is a hide-a-bed & she hands over
a set of keys.

Outside the motel window, three steps off
the crumbling pavement at the edge of the parking lot
is a drainage canal filled with moss & two ducks
nibbling at crawdads. Sunset sits
on the embankment & smokes a Lucky Strike.
Twenty yards across, a dead-end street
(the yellow diamond sign eroding
in the shallow municipal water).
Bikes lie in yards, their reflective disks
winking into the night. Down the embankment,
two armadillos roll out of the storm drain. Sunset
smiles at the end of the road as the final
ember pulls itself dimly into his lungs.

Gentle, he mentions the Y-shaped scar bolting
down the Perfect Bastard's right cheek.
Comments on how it frames their eyes
funnels attention to their jaw, notes the slope
down to their chin & the curl
of their lips.

He asks & they say yes. They ask back.

Watching the ducks, they run fingers
through Sunset's golden strands, let palms rest
where shoulders swell into neck,
excited blood rising. Still, they flinch
when headlights scan over the two.
Metronoming gaze, swiveled neck,
lock of spine. Somewhere in this mess,

a hand grips the handle of a concealed
switchblade, finger resting anxious
on the eager button. Another hand rests
on a knee, a firm squeeze. Not tense. Firm.
Thankfully, nothing. The first hand
relaxes. Fingers run through hair.
Skin turns gooseflesh. Ducks splash.
Laughter.

Sometimes you see with your eyes.
Sometimes you see when you close
your eyes. Watch how slow
I can run now.

outside
the window
a pickup
truck flashes
searchlights
up across
the high
ceiling

outside
the window
people yell
or laugh
back & forth
intentions
muffled by
double-paned
glass

outside
the window
cold night
sinister shadow
puppets prowl

inside
the window
they lie in bed
& let desire
dream you
-r touch
into reality

in the
warm dark
of the room
under
the sheets
you

slide
your
fingers

just two
or three

over
their
tender
palm
&

no one
flinches
or pulls
away

[NOTE]

You press shooting stars—
hot, pulsing, unheard of—
into my chest.

> *Even if this crowd won't*
> *I'll trace you into the stars*
> *& make you a constellation;*
> *let's write our own mythology.*

Back on the road, the Sunset Kid talks
about landlords / lariats / leases / leapfrogs
over charging foes in the ring. He's tired

of the Sunset Flip. He wants a new move, wants
to hoist his opponent up on his shoulders like
a proud father, let them soak in the crowd
before he presses their spine into canvas,
calls it the Angel from Montgomery.

                              Yes, he's tired
of the Sunset Flip but what else can you do?
What choice but leap / tuck / drop / dazzle /
disappear?

The two wrestlers keep a cooler in the floorboard,
Ziploc bags full of ice. Fill up in the motel before
checkout. Slip behind the small of the back.
Let the cool seep into the muscles that hug
the spine. Let the spine straighten. Decompress.
Alternate with heat. If they had heated seats.
They don't. They imagine dropping Holiday
right on his seat-heated spine. His hometown
tonight. Babyface entrance. Huge return.

Listen to the crowd pop. Hear them sing back
his music. Alternate with heat. Run-in from
the heels—the Perfect Sunsets lurking
in dark hallways, armed with chairs &
bamboo bats. The Perfect Bastard wears
a handful of trinket rings—costume jewelry
& some family marriage bands. Big diamonds
jagged with divorce, death, time. An Irish claddagh.
Hands clutch the heart. A cobbled family history
cracks against the jaw of the prodigal son.

See how those rings flutter in the light
like crooked stars. See how they kiss
their own jewels, praise their own
invented iconography, inherit a history
they rewrite in the ring. Hear how
the crowd roars. Foaming. Boiling. Quaking.
Hear how they sing slurs. How they
invent new names. Historic names.
Murdered, dredged-up names.

Heroes arrive to save the day:
Bankroll Brady in her heirloom earrings,
silver silk, splinters a disco ball
over the skull of the Perfect Bastard.
The Executioner wraps his knuckles
in a thick chain & cuts Sunset down
with an axe-handle chop. Triumphant.
Almost high on the crowd's cheers. Music
hits the speakers. Top of the ramp:
the champ herself. The track skips
& the Cyclone casts a challenge:

THE PONCA CITY CYCLONE & TANNER HART
VS.
THE EXECUTIONER & BANKROLL BRADY

flashes on the screen too quickly,
too cleanly edited, but illusion
can handle the weight of spectacle.

Hart does what she knows &
so does her partner. She chucks
slingblades, suplexes, drops DDTs
& Cyclone snatches a surprise tag,
sends Hart back to the sidelines.

Hart does what she knows: distraction
& when Ponca turns, the Axe is swinging
right through him. The ref slaps three
long before the world stops spinning.

The crowd's cheers carry the babyfaces
back to the locker room while a fake relationship
becomes too real too quickly & Ponca City eats
Hart's unscripted boot. She cuts a promo:

Bankroll, you put up a damn good fight tonight.
Next week, leave the Executioner in the back & fight
me one-on-one for the belt. I'm done waiting
for my chance. I'm taking it & I'm taking you with me.

in the parking lot after the match, the wrestlers
pile beer cans at their feet. Hart holds an iced can
to her temple & sighs, says, *Best match I've had in years.*
Only match I've had in months. I hoped life was more
than stand still & look pretty. More than
"Accompanied by Tanner Hart." Thought I might make a name
for myself, but these days, I just find my name in fine print
beneath a man they're paying me to love & they've never paid me
enough. Every time I kiss him, I think about my wife crying at home
even though I know she isn't. Sometimes I wish she would,
but Clarity takes it all better than I do. It's all business, *she says.*
I understand sometimes you've gotta play their game.
She's trying to be supportive. I know it. But it just sounds
like she's giving them permission to keep me sidelined.
Sometimes I think she likes me better as the valet, not
taking the big bumps in the ring. That stuff's always scared her.
She loves me. I know it. Not always the way I wish she would. I try
& tell her, but words—No, words can't do it. Can't explain
how I felt in that ring, brushstroking my palm across Axe's jaw.
That burn in the knuckles. That stinging. My boot print
in Ponca's gel-slick hair. I can see Claire's eyes right now,
ghost-white & shaking. She hears me & that's what scares her.
But she doesn't feel it & that's why she can see the silver lining
my corporate raincloud. I'm just tired of working against
the system from the inside. Tired of playing ball & hoping
they'll wake up one morning & throw me a pitch. I want
to get in that ring every night & feel the way I feel right now.
Right here in this parking lot, drinking beer with you two
& aching all over. Because that's a kind of love, too.

In light of her recent, unwarranted actions
(on live television no less), we have made
the decision to vacate the Women's Championship
& indefinitely suspend Tanner Hart.

We pride ourselves in providing audiences
with compelling, long-term storylines. Here,
as in life, there are ups & downs. Not everyone
can always find themselves on top of the world.
If you feel like you're stalling, we ask that you
practice patience. Your time is coming, too.

[FLYER, PASSED AROUND BACKSTAGE]

Jobber's Revolt

Every night of the year
in every town on the map,
the boss asks us to go out
& lie down on our backs.

Tonight, we give 'im just that:
Walk out of the locker room,
right past the hallway leading
to the ring & out into night.
Lay down your swords, your
shields, your steel chairs
& lie down in your own bed.

each morning, the sun rises
over banks & bookers;
tonight—sunset

55

The Judge: the Executioner—
mid-card talent playing traitor
to get in good with the boss—
wields a store-bought gavel
like a butcher's axe. *Thunk!*

Jack Holiday: the prosecution
wears the title around his waist
to remind us where we all stand
or, maybe, to remind him
who cuts his checks. He paces the
locker room saying words
like *seditious* as if
he knows what they mean,
talks like he's cutting a promo,
his index finger, thick as a cigar,
in the face of the Kid, in the face
of the entire locker.
*You've got to earn your spot. You can't
demand the world & expect it
to hand itself over.* The belt shines
in the light. He passes around
the flyer we've already seen,
but we act as if we haven't.

We can't take our eyes off
the pearly glisten in his jaw,
the kind of smile that haunts posters
in dental waiting rooms. Someone
pays for his teeth to look like that,
for him to smile big on talk shows,
that much is clear. When he smiles
not a hint of yellow—not gold
or nicotine or plaque. We want
to punch each little pearl into
the back of his throat. We can
picture it, the thick gargle, jangle
of teeth, the long, drawn quiet.

But it's pointless, we know.
Some handsome, affable dentist
would simply replace them.
There's money, always,
to fix those kinds of things.

Outside, Bankroll Brady
fetches a set of bolt cutters,
but she knows. Inside, she sits
quiet, like everyone else,
in their folding chairs &
no one uses them for their
true purpose.
                                Then,
Holiday reads aloud from
notes he "found." Within,
a clear desire for revolution,
a planned, calculated effort.
He doesn't say their name,
doesn't even look their way,
but it puts the Perfect Bastard's
stomach into a full nelson.

In the end, Sunset is found guilty
& ordered to buy a few cases
of scotch for Holiday & the Axe,
but we all know. The real trial
happens behind closed doors.

After two weeks of silence & carrying duffel bags, time finally catches up with the Sunset Kid. *This is my retirement match*, he says each night, patting the Perfect Bastard on the back & heading to the ring. They try to talk to him about the notes: "I didn't give them to Holiday." / *I know.* / "I should buy a lock for my bag or keep it with me or—" / *He would have found a way.* His tone never rises & he never glances away, never breaks from their eyes. Even when he talks about Holiday, he doesn't sound angry. *Big money. The kind of paycheck you might fight to keep.* Rise. Pat. *This is my retirement match* & one night, outside Kansas City, he's right. The Axe cuts him down in a two-minute squash &

that night a knot of strings
pulls Sunset into a boardroom
& then the slow, silent walk
to the parking lot
beneath an orange sky

there were theories—

it was all a work, a planned
comeback just down the road,
big storyline with a nice finish

they offered him the gold belt &
maybe the rest of us could fail
to take it from him if we're lucky

that whatever was said
sent him rushing to the car
tail-tucked & blurry-eyed

there were theories
& the one scrap
of unyielding truth—

      evening
turns to night.

[ACT III]

The Perfect Bastard Dreams of Gold

The Perfect Bastard walks through
back alleys rutted by tire treads,
avoiding pools of discarded rainwater.
Around them, chain-link fences
once rusting & unraveling
have been dipped in wet gold
& twisted back into place. Now,
gates unhook, swing open
without resistance. The Perfect Bastard
steps into a backyard
                     & there,
in the center of the trimmed yard
where once two blue gymnastic mats—
vinyl cracked & stuffing picked away by birds—
hosted adolescent scraps, stands the ring,
the squared circle, four shimmering posts strung
with angelic ropes, red velvet or pure soft gold,

                     & there,
in the center of the ring, a bell chimes,
the crowd roars, the commentary panel
bellows & they are in the ring, holding
in their hands the blinding gold strap.
The weight of real metal that sunk them
then returns in their dreaming, weighs down
their hands, burdens the knuckles,
produces small stinging cuts in the delicate flesh
between fingers where acidic sweat burns
into the bloodstream. They squint, unable
to see past the luminescent band weighing
on their palms.

                     & there,
through the glare, stands their friend,
not grown, not made new, not gilded
but Sammy as he was then—stuck in time,
suspended by guilt, small boy, full of excitement,
back turned, drinking in the swell
of the crowd

          & when he steps down from the ropes,
                              turns
to see the Perfect Bastard, their body begins
to move, their mind tries to tighten their muscles
but it's too late. Their legs take a step forward
& arms swing the glowing, white-hot belt
into the unbroken nose of the tiny child

again.

                         ⌒

It was like lightning:

first the dazzling ray of light
then a silence that stretches across forever
& the loud crack of thunder
as the belt breaks across your face
or rather your face breaks across the belt.
Blood comes the hard way.

You're invited
to a live broadcast
of true love
in the semi-main event

The Perfect Bastard marries
their first & only sweetheart
in a ceremony for the ages

[POSTERS HUNG AROUND TOWN]
THE PERFECT BASTARD & THEIR FIRST CRUSH
STAND BENEATH AN ARCH OF ORANGE-YELLOW ROSES

[COMMERCIAL, 5:32 P.M., LOCAL STATIONS]
Witness history. Witness spectacle. Witness love.

During a Radio Interview on the Night of the Ceremony, Someone Calls In & Asks the Perfect Bastard, "How Do I Explain to My Children All of This Queer Love You're Flaunting on TV?"

& the Perfect Bastard wants to say to the man,

How will I explain to my own children? to my mother?
to my myself? that my love is not a publicity stunt
when tonight, in front of the cameras, it is?
Tell me, sir, dear caller, long-time listener,
how do I tell the world that I am truly
who I say I am when I don't have a say
in the self claimed for me? Sir, did you know
queer love is real? That it wasn't cooked up
in a pitch meeting, that it isn't a desperate
grab at dwindling ratings? Sir, please,
if you know these things: Tell me they're true.

but the Perfect Bastard bites their tongue & reads
the cue card: *Tune in tonight & see for yourself.*

They Say 50% of Marriages End in Divorce, but 100% of Pro Wrestling Marriages End in Disaster

Chekhov's gun, isn't it? To stage joy in a ring
designed for violence & expect violence
not to barge into the rehearsal dinner drunk & sloppy.

Give me a break. Nobody signs a contract
without flipping the table & swinging a few fists.
Certainly no one is happily wed in this world.

No, not without blood. You know as well as me
in this ring, wedding bells are just the same
as the ring bell in the corner—when it starts ringing,

someone is going to throw a punch. This time, it's me—

the beautiful blushing bastard bride, dressed in white,
holding an explosion of pink flowers. Backstage,
I drape a sheet of lace over pink & white face paint.

You lift the veil only to find another veil. Doesn't it just feel right?
My family plays this game during the holidays—
I'm telling you this because tonight I am welcoming

you into my family—& the rules are simple: you take $20
(or $10 if it has been a rough year) & you put it in a box
covered in gift wrap. You wrap that box inside another box

& you wrap that box inside . . . Well, you see where this is going.

You slip on a pair of oven mitts. Someone cranks up
one of those old kitchen timers & you try your damnedest
to rip these boxes open before the time runs out. Get it?

The veil over my makeup. Makeup over my face.
What of this face? What's it hiding?

                                        Tell me,

is it an act of intimacy
or violence to step into this ring

& let men in oven mitts try to rip
back all my layers? What is it

when I'm standing in front of the mirror
doing the same? Don't answer.

There's no time for that.

Tonight is my wedding & listen:
they're playing my song.

Tonight, the Perfect Bastard Is the Sacrificial Poet

Garlands hang from the ropes,
pansies & daisies soften
the corners. Beneath the arbor,

the referee replaced by a man
smiling in his suit. A sign
in the crowd, young woman: CONGRATS!

The Perfect Bastard knows
what's coming, but still smiles
like they're in love. In the ring,

they set the table—
unhook the metal legs & slide
the small, metal latch into place.

They give the table a firm pat
for good measure, inspecting
the durability of pressed wood.

Their palm strikes
the finished surface, a twinge
in the spine—the opposite

of phantom pain, remembrance
of future anguish. Nervous sweat,
wedding jitters. Happens to everyone.

It's impossible not to think
about the life of a folding table.
The seed, swallowed by a robin

or caught in the matted fur
of a gray squirrel, dropped
into some happenstance of earth

or else deposited deliberately
by tender hands & pressed into soil
by green thumbs. The rain.

& then the sudden gasping leap
into carbonated air. Of course,
the axe. Or lightning bolts.

Hands planting & chopping
& pressing wood into boards.
The bolts attaching the legs

& now, the Perfect Bastard
placing the table in the center
of the ring. A smattering

of steel chairs, unfolding,
sliding into place with care.
Look what I made: a home.

Look what I'm about to
unmake: catastrophe waiting.
The rule is simple:

if you set the table,
your body crashes through it.
What an offering, to lay

out an altar for another
& give your body over
to plywood & steel.

The First Crusher Breaks Kayfabe on the Radio

The Perfect Bastard is kidding themselves if they bought
into this farce for even a second. If they stood in the back
halls, oblivious to the man aiming the sixteen-pound
camera right at them, if they never looked up to see that
boom mic hanging low like a rain cloud or a revelation
& let even a single neuron fire with the thought that any
of this was anything more than a straight man's soap opera.

Powder their face & present the Perfect Bastard with their
rainbow wig. Do the same for any clown in the audience
whining about the way life really is. Bring them into the ring
& I'll put each & every one of them through a table, too.
If the Perfect Bastard wants to buy into a fantasy, I tell them
to meet me in the ring & we'll see how many boards a body
can break through before they feel the reality of this world.

The Perfect Bastard vs. the First Crusher II

I've watched the tapes back. Listened to the radio interviews. Tossed the ring into a lake & didn't let the production crew film it for the angle. I've gone through the process of meeting you all over again, which is a form of grieving. I've heard the jokes again & didn't laugh this time. I've ignored the smile on your face & looked right into your blank, patient eyes. Now I know.

You made a mockery of me, mockery of my love. I was the punch line to your big joke & these dimwits in the stands ate it up. You riled up hordes of bigots on Twitter to fight for you, to parrot your hashtags, but they can't protect you when you stand across the ring from me.

In the middle of this ring, beneath the spotlights, surrounded by your fans, your name trending, I'm going to rake my hands across your face / pull back / lock in the Bastardlock / & you're going to tap. You're going to quit the match, beg for someone to come throw in your towel. But I'm going to keep that hold locked in. A live microphone right in front of your face—you love to hear yourself speak, right—& I'll let you explain to me again just exactly how funny your big joke is.

—∞—

they lock collars & elbows together,
tie two bodies into one until it breaks
or becomes something more beautiful

It feels so real, so true & it's hard
for the Perfect Bastard not to smile,
to close their eyes & feel flesh ripple

after a firm chop, hard not to hear
the ruthless snickering of old bullies
on the Crusher's venom tongue, hard

not to meet the eyes of cashiers
fighting back laughs as they deposit
coins into neon-polished hands

hard not to imagine balling those hands
into fists, tossing a storm of dimes & nickels
back into the once-delighted faces

of everyone who ever laughed at them,
ever saw the Perfect Bastard for anything
less than a celebration of the self

& it's hard & it's hard, ain't it hard
not to see all their faces in the ring now
& rake their eyes with nail-polished fingers

they feel alive, time has dropped away
& they're back in the ring with only
their opponent, but *opponent* is not
harsh enough, not anymore

the Perfect Bastard looks to the crowd
& sees only the First Crusher, looks
to the First Crusher & sees only

an arena of hateful faces, laughing
the Perfect Bastard doesn't care
about being melodramatic, hysterical

the Perfect Bastard wants to pull
the First Crusher by the collar
up every row of the arena &

beat him with every chair in the house
the Perfect Bastard wants to set the table
again & splinter it over & over until

the First Crusher can't sit down to eat
without thinking of them   the Perfect Bastard
locks in the Bastardlock, wrenches it tight

across the face of the First Crusher
& there, in that moment, they cry,
let the tears wash away the paint

they don't think about Sunset or Tanner Hart
or Adrian Street   they don't even think
about the First Crusher   No, in the middle

of the ring, muscles straining, the Perfect Bastard
thinks of themself, of their mother, of the shoulders
they sat upon to cheer the faces, boo the heels
& they cry & cry & cry

& it's hard & it's hard, ain't it hard
to forgive the people who hurt you
& it's hard & it's hard, ain't it hard
to love yourself & try to live true

the Perfect Bastard, lips quivering, arms
shaking, releases the hold, & through
blurry eyes, they see the silver bullet

of an engagement ring hurtling for their
temple   looking up at the lights,
they hear the ref's long count to ten, hear
the ring bell chiming, lying still

in the arms of the First Crusher

The Rebirth of the Perfect Bastard

the sun
fully set,
tucked
beneath
the globe

the heart
cratered
by splintered
board

a comet
crashes
into earth
& creates
the moon

but
somewhere
out in space
floats a cloud
of moondust
& fragmented
comet tails
a nameless
belt of asteroids
orbiting
binary stars

until
the pull
of gravity
becomes
too strong
to ignore
& the moon-comet
perfect-bastard child
condenses
into human form

on earth
they moonsault
through phases
of waxing &
waning light
crescent off the top rope
land in canvas
craters, trailed
by burning ice
& glittering rocks

in the absence
of an orange,
burning star
or the red burning
of the chest
the moon's child
creates their own light

burns & burns
in the ring,
meteor showering
into opponents,
blazing through
every season
of the zodiac,
turning all obstacles
into galactic ash

& at the end of the year,
as the planet orbits
the lack of a sun,
the Perfect Bastard
prepares for the Holiday

[ACT IV]

Rose Gold

Backstage, on the walk to the locker room, the invisible strings
tug at the flesh of the Perfect Bastard, pull them into a conference room.

The Puppeteer, Keeper of Language, Bestower of Names,
says *All bastards want is a last name, so I'll give you mine.*
I give you the name Champion & so you'll fulfill that name—
fight for my honor. In my name, forget yourself.

> *I name you Champion*
> *or I revoke all names.*

& is there room to argue?

⸰

Next week
after the bell sounds in the main event
the Perfect Bastard will run to the parking lot,
the championship belt around their waist.

Before that
Jack Holiday crumpled in the ring, sobbing.
The angle just right for the camera.
A smudge of lipstick.

On the ramp
the Perfect Bastard paints the belt rose gold.
Holds a pose just right for the camera.

Pan to the crowd
outrage often simmers just beneath the skin
leaks out the eyes / eyes leak before the lips
but then the (mis)names slip into the air

⸰

> *You're going to kiss a man*
> *& we'll drape you in gold.*
>
> *It's beautiful.*
> *They'll set the stadium on fire.*

& is there time to think?

Jack Holiday Cuts a Promo

at the end of the night / in the ring

the high school gym, bleachers packed, ring assembled atop warrior painted on parquet boards, Jack Holiday walks out of the varsity locker room wrapped in leather & gold. He steps up onto the stage normally saved for graduation & offers this commencement:

You can't expect these people to love you.

The broadcast buzzes through an old TV set, strapped to a wheeled library cart & in the visitor's locker room surrounded by the other heels—murderers, cult leaders, the undead, the unloving, & the Perfect Bastard, the queer—they watch, eyes focused in on the white shine of Holiday's insured teeth, & they listen:

Not the way they love me.

They say that an unstoppable force
& an immovable object cannot exist
in the same place at the same time, so
next week, when we step into that ring,

I'm going to show you
what kind of force I am.
I'm going to show you
that you & I cannot coexist.

Paradox:

if I tear you apart, limb by limb,
at what point are you no longer you?

If I scramble your face & let
all the free clinic's horses &
all the free clinic's men try
to glue your teeth back in,
realign the bridge of your nose,
at what point do they—do you
admit that you'll never have
what I have?

Listen to this crowd
& you'll know: I will always be
the have to your eternal have-not

Listen again:
these people actually know my name
& that's what sets us apart.

The Perfect Bastard pushes off from their folding chair & walks through the door, out into the hot air of the screaming crowd. From a skylight, the softening sunlight falling on the mid-card matches has fully set. Beneath the canopy of celestial mothers & burning heat lamps

the Perfect Bastard walks to the ring,
stares down the man & then the people
who love him, points to the shining golden
moment Jack Holiday holds before them
& next week the match is set. The main event.

& now there's a week reserved for thinking.

Adrian Street Wins the Mid-South Television Championship

[SEPTEMBER 26, 1984
IRISH MCNEIL'S BOYS CLUB
SHREVEPORT, LA]

As his music plays, a small child in the front row bounces along on their mother's knee, clapping joyfully as the crowd shakes their down-facing thumbs at the camera. Street is outfitted in chains & leather, tipped with red & black feathers. [*Look at that man.*] A skull set in the dead center of his forehead, wings fluttering around across the eyes. [*I suppose he's a man.*] To one imagination, Adrian Street has emerged from the heavy curtain in the back of certain bookstores & stumbled upon this ring. But the Perfect Bastard watches a man approach battle, dripped in blood maroon & clad in armor. Adrian Street marches to the ring to slay a dragon.

The bell chimes & Street tosses a swift leg strike, but glides at the last moment, slides the hand up the thigh & admires his own body. He flaunts & postures, skips around the ring. Even in this he betrays a brutality, each dainty hop thundering upon the mat. [Commentary: *His lifestyle is unorthodox.*] The champion Terry Taylor tries to grapple, but Street somersaults out of every hold. Taylor launches Street from one corner to the next, but every time Street pops back to his feet & poses for the crowd, arms spread wide to drink in the frustration of the champ. [*It is hard to describe the movement of Adrian Street.*]

When the ref isn't looking, Street sneaks his heavy, closed coal-mining fists into the face of the television champion. [*A blatant right hand.*] Street braids Taylor's limbs. He chucks uppercuts [*Don't let his appearance fool you.*] & throws his body to the wind. [*He is double-tough.*] Taylor drops Street's ribs onto a sturdy knee, stomps both feet into the chest. He lays in chops & resorts to a closed fist of his own. [*This is a see-saw battle.*]

Street struggles to his feet. [*Street's in trouble! Adrian Street is in trouble!*] Taylor gripping a fist of his platinum hair. [*Adrian Street's complaining about the hair & then* What?] The crowd squeals. [*Oh my God!*] Taylor squirms, fights to get away. [*He's kissing Terry Taylor.*] Street grips the back of Taylor's head, pressing his red-stained lips into the champ. [*I have never seen anything like this before in all my life: a man kissing another man.*] [*Dazed*] Taylor stands [*confused*] shocked-still in the middle of the ring & Adrian Street rolls him up for the three count.

From the commentary panel, Joel Watts screams *I have never seen anything like this before in all my life: a man kissing another man!* but those words could have fallen from the slack-jawed mouth of a young Perfect Bastard, in their bedroom late at night. They glance frantically to the crack beneath their door, watching for shadows to disrupt the thin stream of light from the hall. Their finger hovers on the eject button on the VCR, ready to dispose of the tape at any moment.

Twenty years later, they watch that same tape, static as each man's punches echo through the screen, & what they notice now—what they can't ignore or unsee— is how Taylor desperately tries to wriggle free, more desperate than when caught in any chokehold or arm bar. How he flails & flails. & then the stillness of his body. Outside the ring, Street presses the heavy gold medal against his heart & puckers kisses at the camera. The new champion of all television staring down the TV audience, threatening the same poison, predatory kiss.

& the Perfect Bastard spends the night hugging the cold porcelain bowl.

In the Flytrap

There are corners of the mind where dust collects
& the Perfect Bastard finally sweeps them out.

The Perfect Bastard thinks about Tanner Hart
& the price of gold. The Perfect Bastard
thinks about outrage & wrestlers stabbed
while leaving the ring, thinks about slurs
lobbed like rocks in school cafeterias &
maps the quickest route to the parking lot.

In the flytrap, the Perfect Bastard takes the time
to imagine possible futures, futures that could be
waiting for them, thick glue hugging the ankle—
the filing for unemployment, the reformatting of résumés.
The pulling of small paper tabs on flyers stapled to poles.
The calling. The holding. The waiting by the phone.
The purchasing of suits or dresses, the sewing of
corporate masks, the new face paint. The vague suffering
of instability that follows the rejection of defined, broken-
in suffering.

The Perfect Bastard imagines goats eating their weight in grass
& falling into a pile of napping goats, a dog with a bandana
watching them sleep. The Perfect Bastard imagines cowboy hats
& flannel shirts, crouches to scratch the dog behind the ears.
Out the window, they imagine big pink skies. Out the window,
clouds are gashed open by towers. Christmas lights wrap the bank.

The Perfect Bastard has seen enough movies, read what lies
beneath enough eye-catching headlines—stories about men
who find themselves caught beneath boulders—to know
what to do in the flytrap. The Perfect Bastard is familiar
with the liberating blade, small & functional. They know
how to spit & scrub & remove blood from fabric or carpet,
but they don't know how to waste away in the clenched jaws
of the contraption, how to sink & starve in the gunk of it all.

Time to learn, the corners of the mind say.
Or grab the knife, says the dust.

For the most part, it is quiet. The Perfect Bastard feels
as though they were waiting for someone to come &
drive them out into the country, for someone to release
the hold & let them scamper off into the woods
or to put a slug in their neck right there beside the road.
There are times they would have picked the latter.

Adrian Street Explains the Joke

If you paid attention, it's all a circus act anyway &
who's more fit for the freak show than the bleach-blonde canary
in the coal mine?

You've seen the photo, haven't you? Isn't that why you're here?
The clown stood next to the father / the working men digging
themselves from the earth? The little mole men &

I had to turn into a badger, frothing at the lips. Fight my way out.
I make it all look easy, but don't think it is. Men in grease-stained
trucker caps & unkempt beards squeeze themselves into arena seats &
I'm their worst fear come to life. They shudder at the very thought of a man
standing next to them at the urinal, so I kiss a man on live television.

This is how you whip a crowd into a frenzy. Hate & panic. This is how
you keep them coming back for more. You make them love to hate you
& they'll forfeit entire paychecks just to see you in pain, just to throw
fists & spit smack-dab in the center of your forehead. Claw your way
to the parking lot & stomp the gas pedal. Enjoy the thrill of it.

Terry Taylor never saw it coming—
A grown man in pigtails
tied with ribbons & lace,
turning heel like he'd never imagined.
I plant a kiss on the lips
of a man expecting a fight,
& the crowd boils with hate.

They've never seen anything like this,
never imagined an act of love between
two men. They know between these ropes
only acts of violence are enough
& here I am, blurring the lines.
Years later, they'll call me an icon,
attribute a history of glamor to my name,

but tonight, the announcers tell the crowd
I live an unorthodox lifestyle. There's a laugh:
when I leave here tonight,
I'll celebrate this win with my wife,
kiss her tenderly & our joke:
Your skin is softer than Terry's.

This is how you make it big.
Listen. Find what isn't yours
& take it. Wear it like a costume.
Take it off when you're ready.
Kiss men on TV & kiss your wife
in private. When you're old enough,
don't untie your pigtails,
just sit in a barber's chair
& shave it all off.

For magazines, take a picture with
your father in front of the coal mine.
The joke is that he's just a man.
The joke is that you aren't.

The Perfect Bastard Calls Their Mom

Voice choking through midnight silver
tears, they become a child again
in the presence of the moon. Mother

child huddled together in the cramped
one-butt bathroom of the old house.
Their mother holds the Perfect Bastard

in her arms while they beg her
to make the hurting
stop. To close the wound & evaporate

the blood. Please, Mother. Fashion me
a different life. Take a pair of fabric
scissors, off-limits to curious children

& bumbling husbands, & snip this
moment away at both ends. Resew
the threads of this timeline, seamless.

Let life go on without this moment
& no one will ever notice.

Scientists doubt the existence of water
on the surface of the moon, but the Perfect Bastard
has seen their mother cry.

Just like she cried in the small bathroom
in the old house when they were a child.

Just like then she watches her baby cry
& knows she cannot help. Knows
the Long Road, the Lonesome Valley.

The Perfect Bastard senses it now, too,
what they were told in the bathroom
so many years ago. Their mother

can only offer this:

The moon only appears to change,
shifting through shadows & contours—
the ghost of light, what remains after
sunset—

        but we know this isn't true.
No, we know we only see one face
of the moon.

The Perfect Bastard wades into the river
on a cloudless night, feels the catfish
brush against their legs. Tears wash

their face paint into the water
as they study the intricacies
of their mother's face.

In wrinkles & scars they see a story.
In the river's reflection they see another.

They cast a signal up into the atmosphere.
There is only stillness. The moon
never changes.

The Ghost of Gorgeous George Visits the Perfect Bastard

after Hanif Abdurraqib

Learn this:

You don't have to step foot in any room
where the people won't lay a rug at your feet.
Refuse what does not honor you
even if they hate you for it.

But remember:

Throw them flowers, kid. Show them love
& beauty even when they don't deserve it.

Pipe Bomb // Pipe Dream

The Perfect Bastard walks through the curtain, into boisterous lights. Already, revolution hot on the tongues of the crowd, shuffling, energetic in their seats. The Perfect Bastard floats into the ring, carried by the static of the room & before they even speak, the crowd knows all the lines. Instead of talking, the Perfect Bastard holds a hot mic to the electric & in one voice the audience chants:

Eyes aimed down the hard cam,
we know you see us. Know you know
the chants—Fight forever, right?
Yes, we beg, pulp each other & never stop.
Sell us tickets forever, drape us in T-shirts
& foam belt replicas forever. Pump us full
of beer & rotisserie hot dogs, now
& forever. Yes, we make our desires known.
Hand it over. We desire two bodies collide
& look at how one breaks against another.
We chant & you deliver & they fight
& we buy & you sell & they fight
& we go home happy & you go home rich
& they go home only when a life is done.

For them: a new chant
or an old one—   Go home.
Sleep. Leave just us & the Booker.
Clear out the ring. Then, clear out
back offices & boardrooms.

We, the audience, disavow this arena
& the seats we pack within it, refuse
the lies you sell us,   facsimile of a war machine.
Not while they die in the ring for you.
For as long as your pawns must sell
their own names to finance your luxury,
we refuse even this, our best love.
We wear no T-shirts, pose no action figures,
won't even watch the bootlegs of your shows,

but we will fill the seats
of every house you build.

Picture this:
Empty ring & packed arena.

The wrestlers have gone home,
to rest, heal
                    & we, the audience,
are hungry for blood, so come on,
come to the ring & put on a show.

We paid good money for the promise of wreckage.
We want tables. This is business. Supply. Demand.
We demand tables. We demand your body, the board
of directors, investors, in a heap.

Won't you give us what we paid for?

& then the sun through the window
& then the revolution is over.

The Perfect Bastard Speaks to Adrian Street

School trip to the fair—
a beautiful woman painting
faces & I dug into my pockets,
the depths of my bookbag,
to scrounge up the leftovers
of my allowance

asked her to brand
an elegant butterfly
across my face.

Like this, I said,
showing her a picture
of you I kept in my bag,
one I pulled from stapled
binding of a wrestling magazine,
one I would later tape
to the inner wall of
my high school locker's door.

In it, a butterfly flutters
across your eyes
& down your cheeks.

You're peering down
at the camera, meant
to look intimidating,
but something about
your eyes is so inviting,
like you've been hurt
in the same way that I felt hurt,

in a way that as a young child,
I could not place or name,
but something about the joy
of seeing you spoke to a pain
somewhere.

The other kids shot me glances
before turning back into
their closed snickering circles,

but still I felt as if I had become
somehow like the creature
now calling my face home.
As if the woman at the face-paint booth
had gently coaxed open
the cocoon I had spun myself into,
revealing the beauty underneath
the utility.

At home, my mother flashed
between screaming & crying,
begging me to wash my face clean
& I had no way of telling her:

No / this is who I've always been.

You made me feel like it was okay
to take the mask off, to show my real face.
I thought you might understand, Adrian.
I thought perhaps your father, too,
had stood in doorways while you read
poetry books or sewed clothes & muttered
I should have played catch with you more.

I thought you understood me.
If there was no one else,
there would always be Adrian Street.
I grew up imitating you just to find out
you'd been imitating me all along.

They called you *ahead of your time*
& I see now the future you predicted.

Newscasters cut through the static
on bunker televisions to warn straight people
against going outside, about caravans
of free love / love wins queers pulling
unsuspecting men from the safety
of their pickup trucks & into the street,
covering them in lipstick kisses & glitter hugs.
Through snowy static on the screen
they yank another man.
                              Out here,
in these new open fields, we share bread
& water, walk down the street unafraid
& call living a parade. Out here, no one looks
twice when I step out in platform heels.

The straights call it a wasteland or whatever,
but we don't even have labels for that anymore.
No, we just wake up & go to sleep & somewhere
in between all that we love whoever walks
into our crosshairs. Wild, violent love.

This is the fantasy, is it not?
The universe you call home, Adrian?
A world of predation powdered & pressed.
A world without consent. No,
your universe is no safe haven.

No, fuck your universe, Adrian.
Your world only replaces danger with
more danger, reaffirms the fears
of the old universe. You tell them
that this is what our love looks like
& they believe you.

They've already made up their minds
about us, so why not play into their fear.
Give them something to be angry about.
Give them a reason to press a boot
into the gut of a trans woman or yank
a gay man from his car. Rile up the crowd,
right Adrian?

In the ring you can be anything. That's
what drew us both to the refuge
of the squared circle. You can be anything.
Why this?

In that picture, Adrian, I saw something
in your eyes. Saw you painting your face
in the mirror, revealing something realer
than skin, giving us a glimpse. Saw myself
& maybe you saw me, too. But I see
the truth now. You never took the mask off.

You put the mask on, the mask
that looked like me. Laughed
when you took it off.

That's the difference between us—
you take the mask off to go to the grocery store;
I stand in the mirror & put it on.

I wear the mask to survive, Adrian
& in the ring, that's the real me.
I thought, once, that you knew something
of survival, of the freedom of the squared circle,
but I don't trust you anymore, Adrian Street.

I see the world you come from
& the world you created &
I reject your world the same
as I reject their world. I refuse
your fear & their fear. I refuse
even my fear.

I'm making my own universe. Real love.

For that world, I pray
simply this:

That a car can pull up
to a drive-thru window
in Las Vegas, Nevada,
& not be turned away,
not be trailed for blocks
by mysterious cars,
a dangerous wedding parade.

This, I promise, will be enough.

Supercut

after Lorde

Right before the match, someone in the back presses play on the hype package—the culmination of a blood feud, footage of the water right before it boils—turns up the speakers & dims the lights. On the screen, months pass by in seconds. The first handshake flows into the first punch like it was always meant to be. Shotgun dropkick. Snap suplex. The bass thuds, lands on the ears with each heavy hand. Spliced between the violent overnight rush, the Perfect Bastard & Jack Holiday have a conversation. {The Perfect Bastard: *I'm greedy, Holiday, & I'm pissed off. I worked my ass off for years while guys like you lounged in private dressing rooms & had Diet Cokes delivered on silver platters. When the night comes, I'm not just coming for your belt, I'm coming for your throne, your reimbursed room service, your fresh-pressed towels, everything. I'm taking it all. & then I'll just give it all away. I'm snapping the padlocks on your gates & letting the boys in the back scavenge your bones.*} Bastard Bomb. Chair shot. Arm drag. Cloud burst. Spill to the outside. {Jack Holiday's promo echoes through the stereos: *Unstoppable Force*} Running dive over the top rope. Life-risking tackle. Treat the body like a double-edged sword. {*Immovable Object*} Throw yourself against a brick wall & hope you don't stick. Something's gotta give, so close your eyes & hope it isn't you. {*You & I*} Stare-down in the ring. {*You & I*} Chest to chest in the back halls. {*You & I*} Two bodies breaking against each other like magnets. {*Cannot coexist*} The Perfect Bastard knocks on Holiday's door, adorned with a golden star. {*So when we step into that ring*} Door cracks open & the Perfect Bastard's fist swings with the hinges. {*I'm going to show you*} Holiday laid out. Wine-red bathrobe. Chardonnay spilt. {*What kind of force I am*} Across the top of the glitter, golden star. Across the shimmering name of the champ. The challenger scrawls *The Age of the Perfect Bastard*. {*I'm greedy & pissed off & I'm coming for everything*}

The magic of the production team is that even the Perfect Bastard watches the tape thinking anyone could walk out of that night with their hand raised.

[A NOTE, TAPED TO THE DOOR]

everything becomes activated
the gun goes off, a metal chair
in the hand is never idle,
a people under the gun,
beaten with steel,
sharpen

—even the sun
eventually sets
or explodes

Action City Screwjob

after Ocean Vuong

[DECEMBER 26, 20XX
PIG PALACE SHOWROOM
ACTION CITY, KS]

1

---

[1] Backstage / Jack Holiday fiddles with his hands & waits / for a kiss he pretends / will surprise him / he calls his wife / says *make sure you put the kids to bed early* / *I don't want them to see* / while the crowd steps out / for a smoke or the steam of piss rising off a thin sheet of snow / the Perfect Bastard comes to the ring / in the half dark of the arena / & the ref steps out of the shadows / to whisper in their ear / just in case someone lingers in their seats / *here's the plan:* / *a solid match* / *sell it* / *we'll give you 10 or 15 good minutes* / *to close out the show* / *& then we'll send your ex-husband in* / *you're still in love* / *who cares* / *it'll boil blood* / *& that's when he hands you the lipstick canister* / *that's your steel chair* / *that's how you make a name for yourself* / *make sure the crowd sees* / *when you apply the poison* / *cheat out* / *smile for the camera* / *smile for your mother* / *smile for Holiday's mother* / *pucker your lips before you plant the kiss*

2

---

[2] Children are always doing what you told them not to / or so I remember being told not to / & so there are small eyes darting & then steady & wide / when a fist thrown like a fastball connects / with a father's smile / a mother wraps her fingers around the faces of two beautiful children / but no one covers her eyes / & so she watches because she knows

3

[3] The audience doesn't know a thing / that's the beauty of the piss break & the cigarette / what steam & smoke conceal / here's what they see: / a fist cracks against a jawline / & another fist reciprocates / & two brutes are throwing potatoes / requited balled-up hands & desperate lips / knuckles & lips kiss / & the crowd is watching a fight they don't believe is real / but somewhere cast out into the crowd is a seed / a rumbling in the feet / spreading through the seats like a wave / the inkling that maybe they can get kicked in the face enough times / & still get back up & maybe they'll be given a crown / I mean a clean finish / I mean, look / look at them / they're back on their feet after a blow like that / & the rumbling has become screaming now / fear & excitement / & you can't tell me that the Perfect Bastard isn't walking out of here / wearing the belt / & only the Perfect Bastard & Jack Holiday know the truth / that the Perfect Bastard really is walking out with the belt / just not the way the audience thinks / so for the crowd it's still a pipe dream / & it does feel nice to hope / or worry / & I'm sure it makes a good story: hard work paying off / a hard-fought battle / a well-earned victory / the violent kiss of fists & not lips / & / & / &

/ a superkick splinters & / eyes close / the Perfect Bastard lies down / & Holiday's eyes go wide / as the ref counts.

A Reprise // A Possibility

Yes. Depending on your definition of dying, maybe the Perfect Bastard exploded into glitterdust & everywhere you go for months / years / decades / you'll find them under your nail beds or collected in corners behind the sofa. The Ghost of Gorgeous George pulls Adrian Street's hair into pigtails & sure, Adrian paved roads for the Perfect Bastard. Maybe the legacy of the Perfect Bastard is what remains / what can't be scrubbed clean / what sparkles. In the dusty cardboard archives of the attic, the Perfect Bastard found Adrian Street in photographs & kindly-rewound VHS tapes & somewhere, on YouTube channels with only double-digit views, are grainy videos from up in the nosebleeds, peeking around concrete columns & there, in those sandpiles of scattered pixels, the Perfect Bastard is still fighting. So maybe a child playing hide 'n' go seek behind the couch gathers a handful of dust & glitter & Perfect Bastards into the world.

So here's the deal—
that kid's gonna come through the curtains with a heart full of integrity & march their way into this ring & demand what has always been theirs &

that kid is going to get it.

ACKNOWLEDGMENTS

Thank you to the following publications where some of these poems first appeared, sometimes in different forms:

The Oakland Arts Review, which first published "Ode to the Pink Cowboy Hat" and "They Say 50% of Marriages End in Divorce, but 100% of Pro Wrestling Marriages End in Disaster."

Aonian, where "The Beauty of the Backyard Wrestling League" and "We Want Tables" first appeared.

FreezeRay, which gave an early home to "Cheap Heat // Action City," "Before It Sets In," and "Adrian Street Wins the Mid-South Television Championship." Audio of me reading those poems can be found on the *FreezeRay* website.

This project could not have been possible without the care of Brooklyn Poets, Cea (Constantine Jones), Natalie Eilbert, and all of my peers in their courses. Their eyes helped mold the initial poems that built up this collection.

Similarly, I am indebted to Hendrix College. To Dr. Tyrone Jaeger's senior thesis seminar and the careful dissection of my peers. To Dr. Erin Hoover's insight, enthusiasm, and shared fandom. To Prof. Hope Coulter, whose "Writer as Witness" course provided the impetus for this project and where I produced the original draft of "Adrian Street Explains the Joke," the first written poem of the collection. To Prof. Angie Macri, in whose courses I first brought my love of professional wrestling to workshop. To Jessica Jacobs & Nickole Brown for their thoughtfulness. To the staff of Hendrix's Olin C. Bailey Library, whose access to periodicals, reference materials, and databases allowed me to effectively pursue the niche research questions that drove this project. To Dr. Toni Jaudon for not laughing at me when I asked her to advise my independent study on professional wrestling. I'm sorry I never actually read *Moby-Dick*. I'm also sorry I skipped class to see Paige Lewis give a craft talk.

To Andrea Berthot who read my first teenage attempts at a novel and said, simply, "You are a writer." That encouragement, affirmation has meant so much for me in the decade since.

To Jessica Isaacs and Dorothy Alexander who watered my love for poetry and deepened my love for Woody Guthrie. Thank you to Dr. Karen Schiler and Prof. Rob Roensch of Oklahoma City University for their early encouragement.

Thank you to Todd Fuller, mentor, collaborator, friend. For showing me the ropes, for believing in my vision.

To Marlys Cervantes, who gave me my first break, who invited me to the college creative writing showcases when I was in high school. You gave me a platform, a stage where I could believe myself a poet. It's that belief that's carried me this far.

Thank you to Sierra DeMulder, Melissa Lozada-Oliva, Olivia Gatwood, G. Yamazawa, Matthew Cuban Hernandez, Giddy Perez, Neil Hilborn, Blythe Baird, Donte Collins, and Yazmin Monét Watkins for showing me the power in my voice. In those brief three minutes on stage, because of you all, I get to feel like the world heavyweight champion.

To Quraysh Ali Lansana, mentor and friend. One of us probably owes the other a text. Let's grab lunch.

Thank you to all of the poets who have graced the stages of the People's Poetry reading series. Your work, energy, commitment continues to encourage and invigorate me.

To Woody: if you didn't live and write, I wouldn't have been a poet. There's a better world comin'. Thank you!

Thank you to all my friends, Morgan, Meadow, Timmy, Roth, Rebecca, Mak, Madd, Josie, Julia, Max, Avery, Sam, etc., etc., on and on, for your love and support, for buying my $10 chapbooks and listening to me ramble about poetry and pro wrestling. Special thank you to Madd for watching pro wrestling with me in the dorm common room every week and Morgan for fawning over the hunky wrestlers—it was all research for the book.

To my parents, Richard, Kelly, for always supporting me, whether I wanted to dig up dinosaur bones, catch wild snakes, play basketball, or write poetry. For your constant love. For raising me on Woody Guthrie and around a host of writers, artists, and storytellers. Because of you, I never knew how to do anything else but make art. To Mopsy for showing me how to live my life.

To the staff at Cornerstone and Northwestern University Press. Especially Marisa Emily Siegel who believed in these poems as much as I did.

And, finally, endless thank-yous to Sonny Kiss and Effy, who give me hope for professional wrestling and for queer folks.